The University of Hull
Centre for South-East Asian Studies

Occasional Paper No. 27

Status Mobility in Contemporary Bali:
Continuities and Change

by

Leo Howe

ISBN 0-85958-592-1
ISSN 0269-1779

Acknowledgements

The research on which this paper is partly based was funded by the Economic and Social Research Council (ROOO234087) and by the Evans Fund of the University of Cambridge. It was conducted under the auspices of the Lembaga Ilmu Pengetahuan Indonesia. I am very grateful to all of these bodies. I would like to thank Prof. Dr. I Gusti Ngurah Bagus for sponsoring my research and for his unfailing help and generosity. This paper is a revised version of one that was presented at the *Bali in the Late Twentieth Century* conference in Sydney in July 1995. It has benefited considerably from the comments of participants, and especially from Tony Day, Carol Warren, Degung Santikarma and Prof. Bagus.

Illustrations

1. Front cover: Members of the *jaba* group from Nusa Penida who have become *déwa pikandel* (see pages 19-20).

2. The *kawitan* (origin temple) of the *déwa pikandel* of Corong (p. iv).

3. Tourists taking photographs of the *pedanda* priest during the cremation of a high status Balinese. Note the nine rooves of the cremation tower (p. iv).

The *kawitan* (origin temple) of the
déwa pikandel of Corong

Tourists taking photographs of the *pedanda*
priest during the cremation of a high status Balinese.
Note the nine rooves of the cremation tower.

Introduction

Whatever is happening to Balinese hierarchy and, for want of a better phrase, the caste system, one thing is pretty certain - it is not disappearing. While there has been protracted and sometimes heated discussion in the Balinese newspaper, the *Bali Post,* over the last few years concerning both the significance and the desirability of 'caste' (*kasta*), status, hierarchy and caste are still, at least in part, the abiding concerns of many Balinese. My aim here is to describe some of the social forces sustaining, and in some contexts even entrenching, hierarchy in modern Bali; but I do not argue that the situation has not changed over the last 150 years. Aspects of the status hierarchy have indeed altered and I shall draw attention to some of these.

Although status drives have been regularly reported in the literature (Geertz and Geertz 1975:120-122; Boon 1977:166 *passim*; Howe 1984; Guermonprez 1987; Schulte Nordholt 1988: 277-81) there are nevertheless few detailed descriptions available. In the post-Independence period much has been written about the social organisation of hierarchy. We now have a clearer understanding of Bali in the nineteenth century, the changes that occurred during Dutch rule and the changes that Balinese society has experienced as a result of Independence and its incorporation into the Indonesian state. Despite the problematical nature of Geertz's analysis of the Balinese state in the previous century (Geertz 1980; Schulte Nordholt 1981; Tambiah 1985; Howe 1991), it still provides a vivid picture of some of the ideas and concepts associated with hierarchy (sinking status, divine kingship, the symbolism of ceremonies, *pedanda* priests, marriage alliance, etc). Boon (1977) has demonstrated that caste status should be seen in relational terms, that it is fluid and manipulatable, and that it is inherently out of step with the set of fixed categories (the *varna*) which appear to inform it. Schulte Nordholt (1986) has argued that in the contemporary period hierarchy is in part the outcome of the way Balinese society was re-structured by the Dutch, and that today it is a more rigid system than it was in the pre-colonial period.

Up to a point this is a convincing argument. Schulte-Nordholt and Vickers are surely correct that the Dutch tried to 'freeze' caste (Vickers 1989:146). The Dutch neither understood nor much liked the complex nature of Balinese hierarchy and for administrative purposes wanted to simplify it by allotting a fixed place to everyone. In particular they were concerned to mark a clear distinction between the upper three castes (*triwangsa*) and the large residual population who were all classed as *sudra* despite the many differences between them (Schulte Nordholt 1986:31), and thence to prevent movement between these categories. As Vickers notes, this in itself created an intense struggle for status since many Balinese wanted to get themselves classified in the high-caste groups before the door was closed on them, primarily because those who could prove they were of high status were to be exempt from corvée labour. But the only route open to them was through the courts, hence the joke about *gusti ponnis* ('verdict *gusti*') that is, commoners trying for high status titles (Schulte Nordholt 1986:37). However, subsequent events allowed the door to be re-opened. When colonial rule ended there was a 'great outpouring of commoners' dynastic genealogies' as 'Balinese developed a new awareness of their origins' (Vickers 1989:164). In keeping with the nationalist and democratic ideas that began to influence people this was partly an attempt to establish Bali-wide descent group organisations to challenge the 'feudal' aristocracy who were viewed as having formed an unholy alliance with the Dutch so as to retain their exalted positions. But it was also fuelled by the pent up frustrations of commoners who now saw the opportunity to activate dormant claims to higher status. Boon notes that in the Tabanan region this manifested itself in *gagus* groups (there classified as *sudra*) trying to reactivate 'lost' *déwa* origins by seeking bogus *prasasti* (genealogical charters) from *déwa* groups in eastern Bali who were willing to fabricate them for a price (Boon 1977:166-7). In other words, with the

2

Dutch colonial yoke overthrown and the 'traditional' rulers unable fully to reassert their dominion, it once again became possible to engage in status climbing. If the Dutch re-organised Balinese society and made caste more inflexible, events after World War Two conspired to loosen it up again, and the tensions that accumulated in the colonial period have since found an outlet in a resurgence of forms of social mobility. In the colonial period the high priests (*pedanda*) presiding in the Dutch law courts made social mobility very difficult; once the Dutch had gone such mobility became possible because, as Balinese in Tabanan said, 'now there is no law against it' (Boon 1977:166).

Today, although under attack from various quarters, caste appears as a ranked hierarchy of named (or titled) groups of people who are related by patrilineal descent (real or fictive) from a founding ancestor, often mythical. The origin of the group, its *kawitan*, is commemorated in a temple in which the living members of the descent group worship their purified and deified ancestors. These title groups are classified, more or less vaguely, by reference to the *varna* categories imported from India, and in Bali known as *warna* or *bangsa*. The *brahmana*, *satria* and *wésia* are known by a variety of terms: *triwangsa*, *wong jero* (insiders) or *anak ménak*; Geertz regularly refers to them as 'gentry'. They comprise some six to ten per cent of the total population of Bali, though in lowland villages they may constitute as much as twenty-five per cent. Related to the *warna* categories, especially the *satria*, are many groups with different titles, *kawitan*, and prerogatives, and many of them are engaged in vigorous status competition with their closest rivals. Excluding Muslims and other small minorities, the rest of the population, the 'commoners', *wong jaba* (outsiders) or *sudra*, are also members of descent groups, but though these are named, the names are not used as titles (except for a couple of exceptions). Ideologically the *triwangsa* comprise the descendants of nineteenth-century rulers who may still be powerful in village and supra-village affairs; others are descendants of minor gentry, and in contemporary Bali all that

3

is left to them is their title, their pretensions and an ancestry linking them, by sometimes devious routes, to an illustrious origin in the past.

A pervasive legend binds the high status groups together. In 1343 a putative Javanese invasion brought the rulers of the Javanese Majapahit dynasty to Bali where they set up a palace first in Samprangan, then in Gélgél and finally in Klungkung. The myth relates that this nobility carried with them the culture of the Javanese court, its etiquette, protocols, art and music, and so forth.[1] One of the later kings, Dalem Baturenggong, is credited with uniting the island into a single political entity and his kin and servants ruled the regions of Bali in his name. Status was calculated by reference to genealogical proximity; as genealogical distance increased so status declined. Groups could also drop status by repeated hypogamous (*nyerod*) marriages, by judgement of the ruler as a consequence of a misdeed or an insult, and by defeat in regional wars. Over time many groups lost status which allowed them later, when conditions were ripe, to 'remember' and re-claim 'original' positions. Alternatively, commoners were often employed as administrators in noble courts and derived prestige and prerogatives from these occupations, but when the Dutch removed these hard won privileges, on the grounds that they did not possess high status titles, they strived to maintain them by claims to higher ascribed status.

While it cannot be doubted that hierarchy was and still is a dominant aspect of Balinese social relations, it is necessary to note also that ideas of collective equality temper this hierarchy. We have very little evidence of the ways in which equality was manifested in pre-colonial Bali other than the now discredited idea that Balinese villages were little 'republics', and that those Balinese residing in the mountainous areas of the island had a more egalitarian social organisation than those close to the courts.[2] However, since the turn of the century, nationalist and communist movements, and ideas of democracy, equality and meritocracy, have led to the formation of organisations and political parties which have sought to challenge the old aristocracy.[3] Anti-caste movements, originating in north Bali, argued that education is at least as important as birth.[4] Land reform and other measures have removed some of the supports to the *triwangsa* and in many places this has resulted in village organisations in which all villagers (high and low caste alike) have equal rights and obligations, and those who try to set themselves above others are vigorously resisted and denounced.[5]

I have argued elsewhere (Howe 1989) that the upper three *warna* tend to be more preoccupied with status than the commoners, but probably this oversimplifies the situation. It is more likely that both equality and hierarchy are always present, but in different contexts and with different emphases. It still seems to me nevertheless that in areas where *triwangsa* are concentrated (largely in the lowlands and in proximity to the noble courts) status concerns are more elaborate and comprehensive, while in the upper and more central regions, where few high castes reside, status rivalry is somewhat attenuated. In such areas one finds some quite remarkable and conscious expressions of status suppression and pervasive ideologies of equality (Howe 1980: 16, 22, 314). However, even here hierarchical values emerge quite conspicuously as core village groups try to gain ascendancy by marrying closer kin (first cousins rather than second cousins; Boon 1977:133) than more marginal villagers would dare to; as they ubiquitously use notions of 'bigger' (*gedénan*) and 'higher' (*duuran*) to distance themselves from others; and pre-eminent village dignitaries appear to be engaged in covert status assertion whilst publicly endorsing egalitarian rhetoric (Howe 1989).

Nothing better demonstrates the continuing saliency of hierarchy in the contemporary period than the many attempts at upward status mobility that occur all over south Bali. But the three cases to be described below also show that claims to higher status can be vigorously resisted by others using a discourse of relative equality; it is the dynamic tension between hierarchy and equality which generates some of the turbulent social forces now pervasive in what is a rapidly changing society.

The '*Déwa*' of Genteng

The first case I describe concerns the *banjar* of Genteng (all *banjar* and village names, with the exception of Pujung, are pseudonyms) in a village in Tabanan. Until the mid-1960s Genteng had been an all *jaba* ward, but then a group of about thirty families began to call themselves by the title *guru*. The rest of the *banjar* was offended and considered the *guru* ambitious and arrogant. The *guru* said they had a right to higher status given to them a long time ago by the raja of Tabanan, and they possessed a *prasasti* to prove it. The *jaba* stopped speaking to the *guru* except when necessary and the *guru* stopped worshipping at the *pasek gélgél* temple where previously the whole *banjar* had collectively prayed. *Jaba* became increasingly angry over this state of affairs and pointed to the obvious fact that all the tax bills, school registers, identity cards and so forth, recorded these *guru* as having *jaba* names. They had always been addressed with *jaba* birth order names, and fathers and mothers were known by the usual *jaba* terms of *bapa* and *mémé*, as opposed to the high caste terms of *aji* and *biang*.

But the real problems began later when, around 1978, the *guru* began to claim they were *déwa*, a fairly high *satria* title. As a result there were arguments in public and antagonists nearly came to blows as *déwa* insisted on their right to be spoken to using more refined (*alus*) versions of the language and the *jaba* refused. The *déwa* maintained their membership of the *banjar* but always sat as a group separated off from the others; they participated in collective labour (*gotong royong*), but again as a separate group, and sometimes performed their tasks on a different day.

Around 1990 things came to a head. The two sides were completely separated; they sat and ate at different food stalls, hardly communicated at all, and apart from cremations were not invited to each other's celebrations. There have been no marriages between the two groups since the conflict began. The *déwa*, valuing their membership of the *banjar*, reluctantly took part in the cremations of the *jaba* group doing only what was obligatory, but they had not themselves cremated any of their own dead in the previous twenty years.

According to the *jaba* this is because the *déwa* do not really know what to do. *Déwa* in other *banjar* of the village, themselves offended, have not volunteered to help them. Not knowing what offerings to use, or what sarcophagus to make, or how many roofs to build on the bier, all of which provide a very good indication of a group's status position, they have simply decided not to cremate. Moreover the *jaba* would probably not assist and might very well sabotage any cremation the *déwa* decided to carry out.

The situation became intractable and the governor (*bupati*) of Tabanan was called in to adjudicate. When asked what proof the *déwa* had to substantiate their claims they showed him a *lontar* (palm-leaf manuscript) given to their ancestors by the *raja* of Tabanan last century, and claimed it was a *prasasti* which proved they were *déwa*. They were instructed to take it to a *pedanda* in Klungkung to have it authenticated. Several members from both sides went to Klungkung and the *lontar* was read. It was pronounced not to be a *prasasti* at all, but a *pengéling-éling* (from *éling* - to remember). It did not say that the group were *déwa*. In fact when people were named, they had *jaba* names. Only a *prasasti* recording the genealogical history of the group as *déwa* could be accepted. The *pengéling-éling* was indeed given by the *raja* but it merely recorded services faithfully and reliably rendered, and it acknowledged and commemorated these. The service given was that of palanquin bearer; wherever the *raja* had travelled it was from this group that his carriers were chosen. In other words the *déwa* were really just servants, and the *jaba* felt they had been vindicated.

Despite this outcome the situation has remained what it was in 1990 and has thus reached an impasse, which is not surprising given the strength of feeling on both sides and the difficulty that external agencies have in trying to exert influence in *banjar* affairs (Geertz 1983:178-9; Warren 1993:43-54).

What sparked off this status drive was almost certainly a gradually accentuating material difference in the wealth and positions of the two groups. From what everyone said it appears that the *déwa* comprise a number of professional people who had become much better off than the rest of the *banjar*. Many are government employees, some have profitable businesses; they own cars and have ploughed money into refurbishing their houses and house temples.

There seems little doubt that status drives such as this one are linked to what people see as a discrepancy between their ascribed ritual status as indicated by their title and their achieved prestige as shown by their material wealth, or as Boon (1977:184) has pithily put it, between 'pragmatically earned versus divinely endowed status'.

On the other hand what irritates and so offends the rest of the *banjar* is the bald-faced presumption of some members to place themselves categorically above the rest and thereby to threaten the relations of collective equality which are today a cornerstone of *banjar* social life. While some *banjar* accord *triwangsa* members certain privileges (for example, they are not forced to assist in carrying the body of a *jaba* since this would place them physically under the corpse), the *banjar* is essentially an egalitarian and democratic institution. At meetings all members, whatever their status position, sit at the same level, they all have the same rights to speak and vote, they speak the same level of the language, subscriptions and other dues are the same for all as are labour obligations. Probably the most important function of the *banjar* is to assist equally in the cremation of its members.

Given such considerations Warren has pointed out that the emphasis on hierarchy has de-centred these other important aspects of Balinese society. While Geertz sees the (royal) cremation as the key symbol of status inequality and aggressive status assertion (1980:117), Warren notes that 'cremation symbolism speaks to fertility, cyclic renewal, and balance in Balinese cosmology as much as it does to purity, power and status inequality of Indic hierarchy' (1993:83). If at one level cremation is infused with hierarchical values, at another it is pervaded by values of equality. She goes on to argue that the occasional disruptions of death ceremonies in which the vehicles taking the corpse to the graveyard are violently jostled and partly or wholly destroyed, and which sometimes even extend to maltreatment of the deceased (Connor 1979), are expressions of antipathy to the hierarchical order, and that status inequality and corporate egalitarianism are 'competing frames of reference around which Balinese culture revolves' (1993: 80, 83); a complete analysis requires that both be taken account of, and that neither should be privileged over the other.

While endorsing the general thrust of the argument concerning the war between *homo hierarchicus* and *homo aequalis*, I hesitate to interpret disrupted death ceremonies as a strike specifically against hierarchy, though this sometimes may be the case.[6] It is clearly on the occasion of a cremation that the *banjar* can most forcefully and finally deliver its judgement of the dead person and/or his immediate family. This is probably why the *déwa* group of Genteng is unwilling to initiate any cremations since it suspects, with good reason, that the whole thing would be a fiasco. Playing with the cremation tower (*ngarap wadah*) or the body (*ngarap bangké*) should be boisterous and noisy[7] even when the deceased was a respected and well-liked person, and there is often a kind of tug-a-war when the corpse is entered into the *wadah* signifying, so I was told, the ambivalent feelings of the *banjar* at having lost a valued member but wishing to speed him on his way to the next world.[8] When the playing becomes excessive the cremation turns into a thinly disguised protest. This may be directed specifically against the character and behaviour of the deceased or it may be an oblique way of censuring the group to which he belonged. In either case this is not necessarily an attack on hierarchy but rather an expression of hatred against the individual or of disapproval against his group for making an unjustified and unacceptable claim to a status position above that which has general assent.

Status and wealth provide privileges but they also carry obligations. Those who are rich, powerful and enjoy high status must be socially accessible, distribute their wealth in lavish ceremonies and feasts, treat people with respect, and be prepared to participate equally with all the other members of the *banjar* irrespective of their status titles. Failure to do so gets one branded as arrogant, cold (*nyem*) and mean (*momo*) and generates strong emotions which may be violently expressed at the burning. In the context of cremation if hierarchy itself was the target of abuse (as it certainly is in other contexts) then such disrupted cremations would be the rule not the exception, and the character of the deceased would be largely irrelevant. In fact what is at issue most of the time is the discrepancy between the expectations of the *banjar* concerning the dead person or his group and the manner in which either of these have practically behaved.

The *Ngakan* and *Déwa* of Corong

Much of the writing on status mobility during and shortly after the colonial period concentrates on the attempts made by commoners to gain entry into high status groups, the main reason given being the desire to avoid the onerous obligations of forced labour for the Dutch. But this argument does not address the issue of those already enjoying high status attempting to raise themselves even higher.[9] Their status aspirations were not based on the avoidance of corvée labour since they were already exempt. It is clearly the case also that status climbing was a function solely of the prestige attached to high-caste titles, and this must surely apply equally to both commoners and *triwangsa*.

My second example is about just such a case since it concerns status rivalry between two *triwangsa* groups, the *déwa pikandel* and the *ngakan*, in Corong, a village in Gianyar. These two groups occupy places somewhere in the middle of the hierarchy. *Brahmana, cokorda* and *anak agung*, all well represented in the village, are usually considered higher than

10

both, though *dewa* and *anak agung* dispute the extent of the differences between them, while *sang* and *gusti*, who are sparsely represented, are generally placed below them.

Starting sometime after Independence some *ngakan* began to call themselves *dewa ngakan* or *predewa*. They began to name their male children *dewa* instead of *ngakan* as before, and their female children *desak* instead of *sang ayu*. Some *ngakan* maintain they have always done this, and that these forms of address are very old and they have a perfect right to them. Others say these terms of address are presumptuous and unseemly. The *dewa pikandel* became incensed because the new *ngakan* names coincided exactly with the forms of address that *dewa* were known by; that is, *dewa* for men and *desak* for women. The *ngakan* thus obliterated one distinction between themselves and the *dewa*. Of course the difference between the two groups is not confined merely to names. *Dewa* consider themselves to be *satria dalem* which means they see themselves as descendants of the Klungkung ruling dynasty, and as entitled to nine roofs on their cremation towers. *Anak agung* repudiate this and argue they should have only seven roofs, which is the number that *ngakan* are expected to use. Nevertheless *dewa* are buried just downstream of *anak agung* and a long way upstream of *ngakan* who are interred alongside *sang* and a little upstream of *gusti*, these placements giving an approximate idea of status distinctions.

The response of the *dewa* to the *ngakan* name change was to change their own name. This they did by holding a meeting in the group's *kawitan* temple in Corong around thirty years ago during which the *dewa*'s *prasasti* was consulted and it was agreed they could change the names of all new born children to *dewa gede* for males and *dewa ayu* for females. This allowed them to reinstitute the distinction that had been eliminated by the *ngakan*.

Both the *dewa* and *ngakan* groups are quite large. The former live in fourteen houseyards in one *banjar* of the village; the latter occupy some thirty houseyards in two other *banjar*. Whilst the *dewa* constitute a single unified group (*dadia*) with

11

its own *kawitan* temple on collectively owned land, the *ngakan* are divided into several groups with *kawitan* either in Corong or in nearby villages. Neither group is particularly influential in village affairs since most of the political and religious functionaries are *cokorda, brahmana* or *jaba* with the former two in all the most powerful posts. Within each group there are very noticeable differences in material wealth, but whereas the *déwa* have acted as a group, only some *ngakan* have attempted to raise status.

Whilst *déwa pikandel* (from *andel* meaning 'reliable', 'trustworthy') is an honourable title, that of *ngakan* is more ambiguous. *Ngakan* is a shortened form of *pungakan* and means 'chipped' or 'broken', usually of a knife, or the piece that has broken off; Barber (1979:619) uses the phrase 'a chip off the satriya block'. Usually *ngakan* are described as the descendants of a liaison between a *raja* and a woman of dubious origins (often a *jaba*). Friederich, writing in the middle of the nineteenth century, says that *pungakan* are *satria* with much *sudra* blood in their veins. He also notes that Déwa Manggis, who robbed the ruler of Klungkung of his possessions in Gianyar, was an inferior *déwa* known as *pungakan*: this Déwa Manggis, by 'deceit, violence and poison' gained mastery over the officials holding sway, on behalf of the *raja* of Klungkung, in Corong and other villages in the Gianyar area (1957:110, 118, 120). Today many high castes in Corong denigrate the Gianyar royal house (since the 1930s restyled *anak agung* rather than *déwa*) and consider it as 'really' *ngakan*; and it is interesting to see that the same insults are directed at Gianyar today as 150 years ago.[10]

It was often said that nothing could be done about such name changes, echoing what Balinese told Boon about status drives in the Tabanan region (1977:166): it was nobody else's business if someone wanted to do this; it might not be edifying, but what could one do about it? it's just a name so what does it matter? if that is what they want to do - *ya silakan* (Ind.) - please go ahead. In one sense this is true. However, there are many cases in which a group cannot sustain a formal change of title unless it is ratified (*mengesahkan* Ind.) by the authorities. This is because, as in any developing state, people need a range of official documents and names must therefore be constant. Nevertheless, people may use new names informally. In the pre-colonial period local rulers decided such matters; in the colonial period, the Dutch law courts took over these powers; but today groups like the *ngakan* can go a long way before state authority is brought in, and even then it may not be effective. Be that as it may, it is also believed that status climbing will engender ancestral wrath which indicates that while the living may not be able to intervene, the ancestors certainly can.

After death everyone (save very young children) has to be cremated so that the soul can return to its origin and join the purified ancestors (*laluur*). This is a long and hazardous business entailing many ceremonies which gradually strip away the ties that bind the soul to the material world. The dead person's family require information on how the soul is progressing, whether it has reached its destination, and whether it is happy. To obtain this they visit a medium to ask for a revelation. Through the medium the soul passes judgement on them. Suppose the dead person is a *déwa* but his descendants have begun calling themselves *anak agung* (this is a hypothetical case I was given). The family asks how he is and the soul replies: 'all is not well; you say my name is *anak agung* but no-one calls my name. My bones have been dug up, my body has been cremated, and the offerings have been made, but no-one calls my name'. This is the crucial thing. At cremation the name of the deceased is inscribed on a piece of *lontar* and attached to the corpse's symbol, and it is through this that the ancestors can recognise one of their own and can call the soul to them. Moreover, before cremation begins the relatives should inform (*matur piuning*) the ancestors that so-and-so is on the way to them, but if they use the 'wrong' name there will be confusion. If the ancestors cannot gather the soul it will return to haunt the family, causing sickness and misfortune.

Such a process was used to explain why one large, extended family of *ngakan* (comprising four houseyards) had suffered so much trouble over the last ten years. These *ngakan* are the most fanatical and determined in their claim to *déwa* status. Their *kawitan* is about five miles from Corong. Over the years many people from this expanding group have been well educated, and have risen economically. Some have degrees in engineering and other subjects, and have moved to Denpasar and to other places in Indonesia. Many return to Corong at times of important ceremonies, and money is contributed to the upkeep of the houseyard temples. More recently they bought some land in their *banjar* and built an impressive and ornately carved *mrajan agung,* in which these families worship their ancestors. In short, they are rich, have nice homes, many live in Denpasar and have homes and cars there, they are well educated and have good jobs, and they have an imposing *mrajan*, which is exactly how it was summarised for me by one of my *anak agung* friends. And if they have all this then they also want to raise their status (Barth 1993:233).

Their material affluence is in direct contrast to their *kawitan*, which is in a poor village several miles away, it is small and the shrines are covered in moss and need repairing. The people who live there are still *ngakan* but are poor and uneducated; they are the rustic relatives from whom the Corong *ngakan* wish to distance themselves. Since the new *mrajan* has been built, the Corong group has increasingly neglected its obligations to its *kawitan*. They no longer go there when the temple's *odalan* is being celebrated, and often they do not even send offerings.

In the process of improving themselves, these *ngakan* also experienced a series of misfortunes and accidents. A child was born lame and died whilst still young; there were many quarrels, jealousies and gossiping in the houses. Some members were in a state of *puik*, that is, they had ceased talking to each other. One man suffered a protracted and painful illness, though he eventually recovered. But it was two further events that led the family to consult a medium about their troubles. Not surprisingly the first concerned events at a cremation around 1987. The group built a cremation tower which had nine roofs, instead of the seven which *ngakan* would normally have, though it was said to be a small tower as if they were afraid of overstepping the mark. The *banjar* felt insulted by this and when they carried the tower to the graveyard they were so excessively boisterous that parts of it fell off and various offerings were destroyed. Many *ngakan* families live in the *banjar* which performed this cremation and quite a few took part in the *ngarap wadah* and the damage caused to the tower, indicating that there was a good deal of displeasure, not just amongst the *jaba*, but also among other *ngakan* who were content with their lot. The particular individual involved here had not, during his life, given people much cause to dislike him and so his effigy (since the corpse was not disinterred) was not maltreated. It was the flaunting of the nine-roofed tower which angered people and which thus received the brunt of the protest. It was impossible to turn back to build a new *badé* and make new offerings, so they went ahead and finished off as best they could.

The other event, which occurred in 1990, was even more disastrous. An influential male member of the group was crossing a busy road when he was hit by a truck and seriously injured. He was in hospital for two weeks before he died. This is a 'bad' death known as *salah pati*.[11] Such deaths are never 'accidents'; instead they are sure signs that something is amiss. The death in itself ensured a visit to a *balian* to see what lay behind it, that is, what made the truck hit the man?[12] The revelation, *raos*, said they had been negligent towards their *kawitan* and their ancestors, who had therefore become angry. The killing was one of many signs they had sent over the years to get their descendants to mend their ways. They were ordered to pay far more attention to their real *kawitan*, pray there more regularly, make sure offerings were sent, and of course, prepare a major set of offerings to make up for the previous lack of respect. Since this happened there has been something of a split within the group. Some members have returned to their *kawitan*, thus implementing the ancestors' instructions, whilst others have continued to stay away. One friend told me that it was rumoured that they were also trying to get hold of the *prasasti*, still kept at their *kawitan*, install it in their new *mrajan* instead, and by this method establish their *mrajan* as a new *kawitan*.

This status drive is not a peculiar and merely local affair. I visited many of the villages within a five mile radius of Corong and discovered that wherever *ngakan* lived at least some of them had adopted the same kind of name changes which I had encountered in Corong. Equally, the *déwa pikandel* group is not confined to Corong, and again I learned that these *déwa* in other villages were implementing the same changes in the names of their children, that is, to *déwa gedé* and *déwa ayu*. In travelling to various parts of south Bali, and in discussion with many Balinese, there is frequent mention of *ngakan* on the rise. In 1993 the *Bali Post* newspaper published a story about a group of *ngakan* on the island of Nusa Penida, just off the south coast of Bali. The article concerned several families of *ngakan* status in the village of Sompang who had begun calling themselves *predéwa*. The governor (*bupati*) of Klungkung (under whose jurisdiction the island falls) had been called in to ratify the change, but so far he had refused to countenance it. He argued that he could not forbid such a change so long as it was only a change of name and did not include a change of their descent origins (*warih*). He noted that indeed the *ngakan* are descended from *predéwa*, but are now *ngakan* because in the past they 'slipped caste' (*nyerod*) several times. According to the governor it is not a light matter to change one's title like this. It must not be done on the wishes of the individual or on those of a sectional interest. It requires the whole village to agree to it and for it to be authenticated by the ancestors (*purusa*). Only then can the governor ratify the change. The process of discussion must be carried out very carefully otherwise there is a good chance conflict will arise within the village (*Bali Post*, 12.4.1993). Three days later a *ngakan* living in Denpasar wrote to the newspaper, quoting Covarrubias (1937:56), and asking what all the fuss was about since basically *ngakan* and *predéwa* are at the same level in the hierarchy, thus contradicting what the *bupati* had said about the relationship between these two titles

Attempts to raise status are fairly pervasive, and clearly the preoccupation with hierarchy is still remarkably strong in Bali. Raising status however is a complicated business and involves not merely the people trying to establish the change, but also the authorities, other people of different groups in the same *banjar* and village, and, just as importantly, a group's ancestors. If it proves difficult to mobilise all these interests in the same direction, the attempt may well be sustained, but at some considerable cost to those who are caught up in it. Moreover, in the two cases discussed so far a number of material factors have been highlighted which appear to play a significant role in the process. Wealth, education, occupations, and such like, can produce a situation in which a group feels that its ritual status is out of step with its material accomplishments. The beautifying of homes and the building of elaborate family temples, the ownership of cars and the experience of the good life, combine in such a way as to generate a discrepancy between the successful, cosmopolitan group and their backward, poor and rustic relatives. The relatively large gaps that are thereby established encourage some to try to break away by disassociating themselves from those they once used to be at one with, and to close the gap between themselves and those above them. This may set off a chain reaction, as we have seen, in which other groups fight to maintain distinctions of rank they see being gradually whittled away, or fight to retain collective equality when status distinctions are being introduced where none previously existed.

However, there are other aspects to raising status. In this and the previous case the reader could be forgiven for interpreting the status game in a cynical way. But there are cases in which, whilst status augmentation is agreed to, nevertheless the group with the new title decides not to use it for fear of creating turmoil.

From Commoner to Gentry

The final case involves a group of *jaba* from Nusa Penida, an island off the south coast of Bali, who 'discovered' themselves to be *dewa* but who subsequently did not insist on all their newly won status prerogatives being observed, both to prevent alienating their *jaba* neighbours and because it would also have *established* a disjunction between ascribed and achieved status when previously none had been present.

Whilst in Corong I met a youth, Putu by name, whose home was in Nusa. He was boarding in a *dewa* household and going to school in the village. It transpired that he was a member of a *jaba* descent group in Nusa which had only recently been admitted to the group of *dewa pikandel*. The Nusa group was very poor and they were reticent to call themselves *dewa* for fear of being considered arrogant (*sombong*).

How had it come about that a *sudra* group in Nusa had suddenly discovered themselves to be *dewa*, and that their *kawitan* was in Corong? I knew that the *dewa* had off-shoots in several areas of south Bali but not that any existed on this island. Putu gave me an explanation. In the distant past some *dewa* fled from Bali to live in Nusa Penida because one of them regularly insulted (*misuh*) other villagers. When his family reached Nusa they became *sudra* like everyone else there, and over the generations they forgot they were *dewa*. Because their ancestors were not receiving due deference they began to blight the family. One man became so ill he almost died. He was taken to a *balian* who, via trance, gave them a revelation. This explained the ill-fortune as caused by his family members having forgotten their true ancestors. Later something very strange happened. A *lontar* suddenly appeared in the dead of night, accompanied by a blaze of fire, in the man's family temple. It was taken to the *balian* who confirmed that it was a *prasasti* attesting the man's true ancestors as the *dewa* of Corong. The group then visited Corong and they were accepted officially into the *dewa* descent group.

18

Some parts of the story seemed authentic. That villagers could be chased away for persistent insulting language is clearly possible. That they would flee to Nusa is also consistent with other aspects of Balinese politics. Nusa has generally been a dumping ground for undesirables, political opposition, defeated enemies and the like (Holt 1970:67; Covarrubias 1937:47; Wiener 1995:45-6), and no doubt this partly explains the island's unenviable reputation as a source of disease and powerful black magic. That misfortune besets those who forget their origins and who therefore worship at the wrong shrines (*salah kawitan*) is also a well-known theme of Balinese culture.

On the other hand the story also seemed preposterous. That *lontar* (and other magically imbued objects) suddenly appear in this fashion is a common mythical theme, but that they become the basis for discussion with sceptical groups who have to be convinced of their authenticity is far less probable. Possibly the *prasasti* was fabricated (Boon 1977:167; Vickers 1989:147). But if so, why and when was it done, and why would the Corong *déwa* be taken in by it? But the most telling argument against fabrication is simply that the Nusa people did not appear to want to gain anything, other than peace and health, from this status leap. These people were evidently not conscious status seekers. It was transparent from Putu's description of life back home that although they were now *déwa*, they did not attempt to draw deference from their low-caste friends and neighbours. Indeed they would appear to be worse off, at any rate in a material sense, because they were now obliged to celebrate life crisis rites with larger and more expensive offerings than previously, and had to bear the costs of annual visits to Corong. Why would they go to all this expense for such insubstantial rewards? Later I visited Nusa with Putu and another friend, and the following account is a combination of material from both Corong and Nusa.

Along time ago a family of *déwa pikandel* from the village of T near Corong were expelled because of the persistent bad language (*salah ngomong*) used by one of them; one man even offered the year 1802 when this took place. They wandered for awhile before settling down in Nusa in the village of K. The family owned nothing and began farming. As everyone in the vicinity was low-caste (*jaba*) they too confessed to this station, and they took on a life indistinguishable from their neighbours. Since it was never used the *déwa* name was forgotten and they came to believe they had always lived on Nusa and had always been *jaba*. They had of course built family shrines and worshipped at these as though they were the group's *kawitan*.

The family prospered a little and began to grow in size; today the group numbers eighteen families, but they remain essentially poor. Their houses are small and in poor repair. The earth is very marginal and yields are low; when the wells run dry water has to be carried in jerry cans some two kilometres up a steep hill. More recently members have migrated for jobs on the mainland, and others have volunteered for the transmigration schemes and begun new lives on other Indonesian islands.

Around 1972 problems began to occur. A series of illnesses struck the group. At a cremation two people were seized by malevolent spirits (*kasusupan kala*) and ran about wildly crashing into offerings and breaking things. People bickered about what were the correct offerings. On the day of the burning the men were unable to lift the cremation tower which is an indication that the invisible forces of the Balinese world were not willing to help. When they managed to pick it up, they kept dropping it and it was a wreck by the time it reached the graveyard. People were confused (*pusing*) and could not understand why so much misfortune had befallen them.

Several representatives crossed the sea to Klungkung to visit a *balian taksu*. They were told they had been worshipping at the wrong *kawitan*, so their true ancestors were angry at being neglected. They had sent messages in the form of dreams and illnesses to get them to act properly. They also obtained real practical information: they were *palarudan* (refugees) and their real origins were in village A in Karangasem, the easternmost regency of Bali.

Some members visited this village but they were not received kindly and no one took an interest in their story. They went home bitterly disappointed. There then followed a series of further visits to other *balian* in different parts of Bali. On some occasions they obtained no revelation, the *balian* being *peteng* ('dark'). On two occasions they were merely told that their ancestors were angry and so they should prepare various offerings. They obeyed but in a half-hearted way, themselves feeling convinced that *salah kawitan* was indeed the source of their troubles. Two other visits had also produced the explanation of worshipping at the wrong temple and one of these resulted in a fruitless trip to a village in Bangli. At this point they decided to give up the search. Having exhausted their cash they were too weary to carry on. Meanwhile far away amongst the *déwa* of Corong the solution to their problems was emerging, and without them knowing anything about it.

About the time of these events in Nusa, the *déwa* group in Corong held the temple festival (*odalan*) in their *mrajan agung*. Things did not proceed as they should have. Described as chaotic (*kacau* Ind.), quarrels broke out, a person fainted in the temple, a woman's tall offering fell to the ground, the dogs barked all the time, and a man was stabbed in the leg by the spur of a fighting cock. As in Nusa it was clear that something was behind all this. It was decided to consult the ancestors in the temple. Through the temple's priest the god told them that long ago a group of *déwa* had fled from village T and gone to live in Nusa, and the ancestors now wanted them back. The god also told them to go to the area of village K in Nusa and look for a man called Pan Meriug who could be identified because he had an eye defect. A deputation visited Nusa to look for Pan Meriug. However they could not find him, but instead located a man called Kriuk who had a squint. The Corong party asked his family to gather and told them why they had come. Each group told their respective stories and it was evident they were *saling alih*, searching for each other.[13]

A group from Nusa then went to Corong where a meeting was held to introduce the newcomers. The whole story was told from both sides. Not everyone in Corong was happy at this turn of events, not really believing these scruffy low-castes from Nusa. After a long discussion it was decided to hold a test. The priest prayed to the god telling him that the *palarudan* had been found and wanted to enter the temple. If they were really 'lost' *dewa* they should be allowed to enter without trouble; if not they should be prevented. As it turned out they entered with ease and the doubters remained silent. The Nusa group were then accepted as true and full members of this descent group.

They returned to Nusa and ceremonies were held to convert their family temple into a *panyawangan*, a 'way-station', so that they could now pray to their true ancestors while still in Nusa. Whilst in Corong the god had advised them not to give themselves airs and graces, and not to boast (*membesarkan diri*, Ind.). To this day they remain very poor farmers, do not insist on high Balinese from their *jaba* neighbours, do not use the title *dewa*, and those alive at the time have not changed their *jaba* names. They have made some changes though. Children born subsequently are now given the high-caste birth order names, and to this is added the honorific *gedé* (big), which is also now part of the names of Corong *dewa*.

Representatives from Corong have visited Nusa several times to instruct them on the making of offerings for major life crisis ceremonies, particularly cremation. They now use a seven-roofed *bade* instead of the normal one roof for *jaba*, and the sarcophagus is a *lembu* (bull) rather than the *gajah mina* (mythical fish) which *jaba* generally use. On the first occasion subsequent to these events when the Nusa group carried out a cremation using a seven-roofed *bade* the other villagers became so angry they threatened to tear it down. An emissary from Corong was sent to Nusa to explain what had happened and after that harmony was restored.

Clearly the most striking fact about this story is the fantastic coincidence it embodies. One group of low-caste Balinese has 'lost' its origins, and another, across the sea and some distance away, has 'lost' a section of its descent group.

22

Through a curious series of revelations and wanderings the two are united, and because of this the low castes from Nusa jump to a relatively high caste position. But this is obviously not a straightforward case of barefaced status seeking, for the simple reason that the Nusa *déwa* are reticent to set themselves up above their *jaba* friends and neighbours. What they were seeking was peace of mind and, in the final analysis, they were not the agents responsible for their elevation; to a large extent they were (willing?) pawns in a game being played by others, but one in which status elevation was always likely.

As mentioned Nusa Penida was renowned as a place for refugees, criminals and exiles, and the belief exists that those banished there were often decasted or frightened to use their caste titles. So it is no surprise when groups 'rediscover' lost origins. Moreover, given that Nusa is home to exiles and refugees, *salah kawitan* is a likely diagnosis for the kind of relentless misfortune which struck the Nusa group. Not only is this an appropriate revelation, it is also of course likely to be accepted with some alacrity by the petitioners, since out of suffering and hardship they find a boon. No longer are they just poor, downtrodden *jaba* of no account, they now have a validated connection to a prestigious high caste descent group in the heartland of south Bali.

In Corong a somewhat similar scenario is played out. A series of unusual and troubling events accompanies a major ritual. Such episodes are always symbolical of something other than their most immediate referents. In the normal course of events women don't drop offerings, people don't usually quarrel on such occasions, men rarely get injured at cock fights. For all these things to happen at once is indicative of something going on behind the scenes, and this can only be divined by gaining access, through a medium, to that invisible world (*niskala*) which reveals connections between people and things that would otherwise remain hidden to ordinary people inhabiting the visible world (*sekala*). *Balian*, spirit possession, dreams, visions, voices from the sky, unusual objects, and so forth are the recognised channels by which people can obtain

23

sure knowledge about things, events and relationships that they cannot get in any other way.

It is less easy to explain the revelation from the god of the *déwa* temple because a number of other explanations might have served just as well. The god could have announced some long-standing neglect in rituals performed in the temple; or that the temple was perhaps polluted by a menstruating woman; or that recently cremated relatives had not in fact reached their destination and were in a kind of purgatory. But, for example, the *mrajan agung* had recently been refurbished and no expense had been spared in doing everything properly. In the end though, it is not possible to provide an explanation for the god's pronouncements. It is true that in such circumstances participants speculate on the reasons for their problems. The possibility that banished kinsfolk is the cause, and that they could be found in Nusa, is not out of the question. It is widely known that Corong, in the last century, was involved in many minor wars and was often in the crossfire of the more powerful and larger kingdoms of Gianyar, Ubud, Bangli and Klungkung which surround it, and I collected several stories in which members of the ruling family and their retainers were booted out of their palace (*puri*) and took refuge elsewhere, including Nusa Penida (see Wiener 1995:242).

The issue of the naming of Pan Meriug is interesting, because some people could not recall that anyone had been named, and one other name, Ampeg, was mentioned. The same is true of the eye defect: there was some disagreement about whether it was to do with the eye, or some other part of the body, and some could not remember it at all.

The general point is that what is remembered is what for the Balinese constitutes the essential kernel of truth, that there was a lost group and that they were found in Nusa, and the details at best are of only passing importance. This was also the case in the account from Nusa. There the details concerning the many useless trips to *balian* were very hazy. Since they were largely false trails there was no need to remember them. When the people from Nusa tell the story they begin by saying that originally they were exiles from the village of T near Corong. But of course they did not find this out until the Corong *déwa* had contacted them. The story as now told is a kind of reconstructed narrative which brings together only what, in the end, turned out to be 'true'. Clearly then the story has, over time, been moulded and shaped to fit the end result. Certain pervasive cultural themes concerning divine revelations, the character of Nusa Penida, the notion of re-uniting long-lost kin, the search for origins, and so on, were acted out in line with, and brought to fruition by, personal and group interests. The coincidence is not so astonishing when one considers that it could easily never have happened, that there are probably various groups of people still 'looking for each other', and that the cultural themes shaping the action also provide various guidelines which tend to engender a successful conclusion.

There is no point in confronting the Balinese with an analysis of these events based on western notions of chance and coincidence. For them what the gods say is axiomatically true and everything else is beside the point. There may well have been other factors influencing the outcome in addition to those which can still be elicited. Nusa Penida is a small island and the Nusa group live only two miles from the main harbour where the Corong group would have disembarked. Nobody knows how long the latter spent on the island looking for the Nusa group, how much difficulty they had finding them, or exactly what transpired when the first contact was made.

Discussion

These examples could easily be multiplied. In Corong the *anak agung* dispute relative status with both the *déwa* and the *gusti*, there is rivalry between the *brahmana* and the *cokorda* (Howe in press), and some *sang* families claim to be *déwa*; and I make no mention of *jaba* groups such as *pandé* (Guermonprez 1987) and *pasek* some of whom claim high caste origins, while others claim origins to other mythical figures who purportedly pre-date the arrival of the Majapahit court. As one female *brahmana* neighbour once put it to me during a game of cards: '*ngakan* become *déwa*, *déwa* become *anak agung*, *anak agung* become *cokorda*, but what can we do?' Another *brahmana*, a well-known wit, chimed in: 'well I suppose we can become *ida bhatara*' (that is, gods), at which everyone fell about laughing. Clearly attempts at status mobility are not exceptional, but rather quite common; but equally common are the attempts to thwart them.

To say something sensible about such processes an analytic distinction between predisposing causes and proximate causes is helpful. The former concern pervasive, long-range, socio-cultural, political and economic forces which constitute an environment in which mobility can thrive; whilst the latter concern the particularistic factors which precipitate a specific claim to higher status. Since material on the latter is embedded in the case studies already given, the rest of this paper will concentrate on the former.

An obvious characteristic of ascribed status in Bali is that it generates a finely graded hierarchy. Disregarding the 'fault line' running between gentry and commoners, which is anyway partly concealed by the overlap in material wealth and because there are very few visible means by which to distinguish people of different station, each group has other groups which are status-near.[14] This entails that all or most groups draw rewards from the system (if one group *renders* deference to a second it can *extract* it from a third) and are therefore willing to invest in it. Because the rewards of status are distributed all down the scale, albeit very unevenly if one compares the top to the bottom, it is only those at the bottom who might have little or no stake in preserving it. Those in many of the commoner groups along with those in the lower gentry are likely to have ambivalent feelings about status. On the one hand they may gain satisfaction by parading their prerogatives to those below them but, in relation to those above them, they may feel that the system is oppressive. It is not difficult to see then that hierarchy and equality battle unendingly for people's

26

allegiances, although this formulation is simplistic and will be refined below.[15]

The close grained nature of such a hierarchy entails an almost obsessional concern with what others are doing. Every time I participated in someone's major life-crisis ceremony (marriage, tooth-filing, girl's puberty rite, cremation, etc) I was cross-examined by the holders concerning the merits of their ceremony in relation to a neighbour's (was the food better, the offerings more elaborate, the assembly larger and more influential, the gifts of better quality and more expensive? the cars more numerous and newer? and so on). Everyone fears being shamed and outdone (*majengah*) by their neighbours and status peers, which thus spurs them on (sometimes ruinously) to greater efforts next time. This process engages an attempt to pull away from others as well as a concern that one is not left behind. It is a competition to introduce or extend differences just as it is a competition to remain equal (Warren 1993:80, quoting Bailey 1971:19). With a rising standard of living for some Balinese new money is being channelled into 'traditional' religious activities, and the poor strive to keep up as well as they can. In Pujung (northern Gianyar) 15 years ago not one of the 225 families in the village owned a gold ornamented wooden offerings platform (carried on women's heads and used to take offerings to temples) - now every family has one, bought at a cost of 200,000 Rupiah (US$100). The lavish redistributive feasts accompanying many ceremonies create obligations which galvanise others to reciprocate, demonstrating that personal prestige is a major element of a status game which has many of the features associated with Melanesian 'big-man' exchange. Moreover status competition is not at all confined to rivalry between descent groups but also finds expression amongst families of the same group. Participating in status rivalry, or being forced into participating, is an important prop sustaining these practices since few are willing to suffer a diminishing reputation consequent on withdrawal.

It is not just status which is important here. One indication of success in such competition is the number and quality of those who turn up at your ceremonies and labour projects, and who in some sense are your supporters. Other things being equal the larger the following the greater the influence and power accredited to the holder. All important beings in the Balinese world have their followers whether these be kings, priests, gods, witches, *balian*, etc. (for example, C. Geertz 1980:24; Vickers 1991:107-109; H. Geertz 1995), but these followers have to be attracted, and all who aspire to prominence strive to increase their circle of dependents. One way of accomplishing this, though there are others too,[16] is to give generously, since this creates debts which can be called in when needed. Nineteenth-century kings and lesser lords secured the services and support of ordinary Balinese because by and large they controlled most of the land. Peasants 'humbly asked' (*nunas*) for access to this land but thereby became indebted to the lord. The interesting twist to this, ideologically speaking, is that people probably gained control of land, and thereby became 'kings', because they were able to attract followers, through kinsmen, strategic marriages, political manoeuvring, etc, to support them (Geertz and Geertz 1975:119-23).

The significance of followers is an aspect of Balinese social organisation which is replicated throughout the archipelago (Keeler 1987; Errington 1989:101-8; Tsing 1990) and it has been pointed out many times that indigenous rulers competed not for land, as the Dutch seemed to think, but for people (Reid 1988:120). Leaders are forced to compete for followers for two reasons. First, because the latter appear unwilling to invest in a single figure and prefer to 'multiply the numbers of powerful people with whom they enter into relations, thereby reducing the degree of dependence they have upon any one of them' (Keeler 1987:88). It is noteworthy, for example, how kings or lesser lords sometimes became jealous of their priests for alienating the affections of their subjects (Rubinstein 1991a:67-71). Second, because land was generally not a scarce resource until recently, peasants could simply move away (*matilas*) from a rapacious lord and attach themselves to a more agreeable one.

There are methods for controlling such competition so that it does not get out of hand. For example, ceremonies should be performed in accordance with one's caste status and with a family's ability to mount it, and there are also village guidelines for the number of guests. (Poffenberger and Zurbuchen 1980:108, 123-5). It is considered presumptuous to exceed these limits, but equally families who put up a poor show when they are capable of much more are quickly branded as tight-fisted. Such levelling mechanisms are indicative of what Scott (1976) called the 'moral economy' of peasant life: those who are well off are expected to help the community's poorer members, whilst the latter have a moral claim on the assistance of the former in times of need. But this is an ideal, and the practice of many Balinese is to push hard against these limits in the hope of 'defeating' rivals. If the poor get trodden on in the rush that is an unfortunate fact of today's world in which dyadic contracts and individualised wage relations come to assume ever greater prominence. I came across several examples of impoverished Balinese who were given the most minimal assistance by their much richer close kin living in the same compound. [17]

Balinese is also a finely graded, hierarchical language which offers endless possibilities for conveying and withholding respect.[18] Nowadays high castes have few sanctions to enforce low castes to use refined Balinese to them, but I was surprised by the pressure on me from commoners to use high Balinese, and by the pleasure which many evidently obtained from using it. Although the extremes of the language are no longer used (commoners told me they would feel grossly insulted if high castes used *kasar*, coarse, pronouns), nevertheless commoners extolled the virtues and beauty of high Balinese. Clearly commoners use high Balinese as much now as in the past (if not more so) because by doing so they can extract it from others in a way they formerly could not, and thereby gain respect. I was frequently told by *jaba* that if high castes wanted respect they had to give it in return. This does not mean that those of high and low status reciprocate equivalent levels of the language, but it does mean that the range used in everyday life has been greatly attenuated. In addition, the ability to speak very good refined Balinese is highly valued in itself; those who are good at it are in demand to sing at temple ceremonies, visit high priests, speak at village meetings, and so forth. The individualistic advantages accruing in this fashion unwittingly continue to reproduce the saliency of the language levels, even if these are now somewhat compressed. Since the language encodes hierarchical values as comprehensively as almost anything else in Bali its continual use is a major factor in the perpetuation of social hierarchy. Balinese remains **the** language of village discourse; children learn it not merely in an intellectual way (as they do Indonesian) but in an emotional way. When hearing inappropriate words they respond emotionally and physically; several *brahmana* told me they felt ill and had headaches if their low-caste friends spoke to them using unsuitable language, and even today very unseemly language used towards someone of high status by a commoner can bring about the intervention of village authorities who can impose a fine and the costs of the necessary purification ceremony. Conceivably one might paraphrase Marx (1970, 1:737) by saying that Balinese imposes a 'dull compulsion of apparently unalterable' language relations, and these relations may constitute a taken-for-granted, coercive reality, which does not require additional verification over and beyond its simple presence (Berger and Luckmann 1967:37). But this is probably too strong since language use is changing and there are ways of sidestepping the hierarchical implications of the language levels (the recourse to Indonesian, for example). Nevertheless, as long as the language supplies most people with opportunities for deriving respect from others it will continue to buttress status rivalry.

The rewards of high status are also material. Whilst many *jaba* have secured high ranking jobs in state and regional departments and bureaucracies, it is still the case that *triwangsa* acquire a disproportionate number of these jobs and tend to obtain the best ones (Warren 1993:273). In Corong all the major village political and religious posts are held by either *cokorda* or *brahmana*; the *perbekel* has been a *cokorda* since Independence, as has the *bendésa*. Villages all around Corong which have sizeable high-caste groups are similar. All the regional governors are high caste, and the story repeats itself at lower levels. Several high-caste residents of Corong have been *perbekel* in nearby, all-*jaba* villages. Moreover, high-caste youth without work in Corong are clearly holding out for state jobs, and until they get them are resigned to being 'unemployed' (some become gamblers, others find work in the tourist sector or obtain jobs in their parents' businesses). In the house (*anak agung*) in which I lived there are no labourers. Three old men make a living gambling, but the rest (eleven people) have 'white-collar' jobs, and this pattern was duplicated in the households of many other Corong high castes. High castes still retain an ideological distaste for labouring work (possibly because it is too reminiscent of the corvée labour performed by low castes in previous eras) which has persisted from pre-colonial days, and which is reinforced by the various beliefs which high castes hold about themselves and commoners, such that the former are more intelligent, have a propensity for scribal work, are more refined, have a better command of high Balinese, have 'brighter' faces, and so forth.

Professional jobs and appointments in the civil service and the armed forces (including also education, health, public works) need not be well-paid to be attractive. The daily wage of a good craftsman can be twice that of a civil servant. But the latter enjoys a number of fringe benefits: security of tenure, monthly rice quotas, pleasant working conditions and an undemanding job, work uniforms which everyone now seems to crave, the possibility of substantial bribes, an early finish to the day, relatively high prestige, etc. It is not at all easy to obtain jobs as civil servants because those responsible for recruitment rarely appoint people solely by reference to meritocratic criteria. It is a constant complaint of those seeking such jobs that they cannot raise the bribes (often at least one million rupiah, that is, $500) that are requested. But candidates also need connections and letters of introduction (*surat sakti*), so that many also complain of pervasive nepotism.[19] If *triwangsa* already have a disproportionate presence in the bureaucracies, and also retain wealth from the past this clearly puts them in a very advantageous position to maintain that presence.

What is so important about these jobs is not merely their contribution to the growing diversification of the Balinese economy, but the fact that they engender their own prestige systems, but systems which are, in part, congruent with caste status. That is to say, the latter provides a framework for the way in which prestige is conceptualised in newly emerging domains of Balinese economic and political life. In almost every bureaucratic office there is a diagram depicting the relative ranking of all the officials working there. No doubt this has a functional rationale, but it surely also reflects the hierarchical preoccupation of Balinese society. Within these offices it sometimes arises that one's boss is a person of lower caste status. Such situations are fraught with problems: what levels of the language should be used to each other, what forms of deference are appropriate, how should relative physical posture be arranged, and so forth? Obviously individuals negotiate their own solutions (the prevalent use of Indonesian, or the reciprocal use of high Balinese, for example, and sometimes the gleeful humiliation of high-caste subordinates), but what is interesting is the provisional nature of such negotiations; and this is now a feature of everyday village life too as people of different caste status 'barter' (*tawar-menawar* Ind.) language forms.

Such government posts provide a variety of material and non-material rewards many of which have an intrinsic relationship to the status hierarchy and the ideas which underpin it. There is a concordance between ascriptive caste status and other forms of prestige particularly since in the latter meritocratic values are only very slowly taking hold. Just as nineteenth-century leaders competed for followers and as they still do now in village affairs, so too do modern bureaucrats seek to attach the loyalty of their subordinates to themselves and displace it away from the organisation.[20] This helps us to understand why the traditional elite seek government posts and why commoners sometimes try to convert new prestige into high status titles. But it is unwise to be too mechanical about this since one aim of the Indonesian state, as represented in Bali, is to effect some reform of caste. A number of government officials (and others too) whom I interviewed expressed the view that *kasta* (caste) is outmoded. Status should not be ascribed by birth but achieved by one's individual accomplishments; it is wrong for the child of a *brahmana* automatically to become a *brahmana* if that child knows nothing of what it means to be a *brahmana*. In short, the titles can stay so long as they are given to those who deserve them because of what they do, rather than for who their parents are. These sentiments are by no means entirely the result of the exhortations of the present regime since they originated in the anti-caste movements of the 1920s (Bagus 1969). However, whilst they are now well entrenched it is sometimes difficult to avoid the feeling that behind the protestations lurk self-interested private agendas, and the resilience of status is still impressive. For example, several civil servants in Corong who made these and similar comments also demanded bribes from job seekers and have been instrumental in placing close kin in lucrative jobs. So whilst *kasta* may be denounced in various official quarters the much greater range of additional prestige systems available today sustains attempts at upward status mobility and continues to ignite status rivalry. Such new forms of prestige both stimulate Balinese status aspirations and provide new channels for their satisfaction, but at the same time they also sensitize others to the inequality of Bali's modern day political culture and thereby mobilise criticism against it.

As I have already mentioned many Balinese attest there is little that can be done if a group decides to give itself new airs and graces. Nothing stops a group building a new *mrajan agung*, splitting off from their *kawitan*, adding two roofs to their cremation towers, using a different sarcophagus, calling their children by new titles, and so forth. Nothing, that is, except the disdain and collective wrath of the *banjar*, intervention by regional government officers or ancestral displeasure. These are of course very powerful forces. But ancestral sanctions are notoriously capricious and inscrutable since their implementation is always after the fact, and in any case may never occur if the group suffers no disasters. Intervention by extra-village authorities gives no guarantee of a satisfactory solution, as others have pointed out (Geertz 1983:179). In a village close to Corong comprising one group of rich *anak agung* (together with a sizeable following of loyal commoners) and a large and poor *jaba* population there has been violent conflict between the two for several years, almost culminating in pitched battles in the cemetery as the former tried to cremate kin against the wishes of the latter. The *jaba*, incensed by the *anak agung*'s failure to take their *banjar* duties seriously forbade them to use the cemetery which is *banjar* property. When the high castes ignored this the *jaba* destroyed initial preparations, sprinkled broken glass in the graveyard and used bamboo spears to threaten the *anak agung* when they persisted. The *camat* (regional government official) has been called in repeatedly to calm things down and to get the two sides to thrash out some sort of compromise but without much success, although the police have at least been able to keep the two sides separate most of the time. This example shows again how resistant the *banjar* is to outside interference, but it also demonstrates, perhaps paradoxically, that for all the supposed resilience and strength of the *banjar* it can still prove ineffective in the face of a sustained and powerful attack from within. The real power of the *banjar* is against the transgressions of individuals, and it is much weaker against determined groups. What price the *banjar* when it is impotent in the face of a group of *jaba* who insist they are *déwa*, as in the Genteng case, or a group of *anak agung* who wish to remain aloof from it? Possibly the Genteng *déwa* will meet defeat when they eventually decide to cremate, but this problem has not stopped the break-away *anak agung*. These latter imported paid labour, musicians and priests, and got their highly placed friends to bring in the police to prevent the *jaba* from disrupting the proceedings. In the pre-colonial period the local rulers, backed by higher status regional overlords, had powerful sanctions at their disposal including banishment, confiscation of land and physical punishment with which to threaten recalcitrant village groups. To some extent state functionaries and Golkar leaders can penalise people by expelling them from jobs and membership. In one such case a man started calling himself *cokorda* and 'bribed' villagers to fall into line, only for him to revert to *déwa* when the *bupati* (one level above *camat*) refused to approve his appointment as *perbekel* unless he desisted. But it does seem that Balinese have as much or more scope for both justifying and sustaining a status drive than they used to in former times.

The wealth and power structure of Balinese society has of course changed in many ways, but there are also continuities with the past. Many nineteenth-century ruling families have lost land and power. They can no longer coerce villagers to work in the *puri*, they no longer have large numbers of tenants whom they can call on, and those they retain are able to strike much better rates of crop division.[21] However, they are still able to wield resources far in excess of most other people. It is said of the *puri* in Corong: *suba gerang buin gorok*, and *berag-beragan gajahé masih ada muluka,* indicating that whilst most of the 'blood' and 'fat' has been used up there is still some left. The *puri*'s *mrajan* still has twelve hectare of wet-rice land for its up-keep and some members of the *cokorda* group retain large holdings of land. The total holding of the *cokorda* group is twenty-eight per cent of the village total. One of them has married a Japanese woman and through her connections has become extremely rich, and with this new found wealth the *puri* has been partly renovated and is full of Mercedes cars, expensive motorbikes, good stereo equipment and mobile telephones and two-way radios. Additionally the core line *cokorda* are highly charismatic. The village will not allow the present *perbekel* to vacate the post (unless another high ranking *cokorda* can be found) because he is thought to be the only person who can get people to do things. Many stories are told about his wayward youth, his ability to frighten those from other villages and so to protect Corong from outside forces, and his contacts with the supernatural. Whilst extremely *polos* (kind and gentle) he is also very *sakti* (supernaturally powerful), and people still look to the *puri* for leadership and direction. By being kind to his supporters and ruthless to his enemies he therefore reproduces in the present the characteristics of the kings of old (cf Worsley 1979:112; Schulte Nordholt 1993:302).

The apex of the 'traditional' politico-religious system was however a dual sovereignty (Guermonprez 1989), with the *brahmana* priest (*pedanda*) being the second part of the axis. Today there is an undercurrent of criticism against the *brahmana* which in some circumstances becomes quite explicit. Some *pedanda* are considered greedy and their houses like shops where they sell overpriced offerings.[22] Many unemployed *brahmana* youth are professional gamblers with a reputation for drunkenness, licentiousness and excessively coarse behaviour; and some commoner groups such as *pandé* and *pasek* have consistently denigrated the claim of *brahmana* to be the highest caste. Nevertheless, in contemporary Bali the high priest's position, while not unassailable, is still powerful and it could be argued that it has been consolidated and improved by events since the nineteenth century. Whereas the old rulers became puppets of the Dutch, the priests maintained their hold on important judicial and religious posts during and after the colonial period, and it was to the *brahmana* that the Dutch turned to gain an understanding of Balinese social organisation whereupon the former were able to advance their own version of Balinese society. With Balinese Hinduism an accepted religion of the Indonesian state and priests heavily involved in writing and authorising many religious pamphlets and organising the huge celebrations at Besakih, particularly through their dominant position in the Parisada Hindu Dharma, *pedanda* have possibly increased in status as *cokorda* and other *satria* have declined somewhat (Howe in press). Moreover, *pedanda* have retained their village role largely intact. Whilst the clients of *cokorda* have vanished or been replaced by employer patronage, the 'traditional' hold of the *pedanda* on his or her clients remains strong. These people still require all the services of the priests that they did 100 years ago (for example, to complete ceremonies and provide advice on offerings, buildings, the 'good and bad day' system, and so on). It is no surprise that *pedanda* are still held in great regard by many, but they are also greatly feared because their curse is so dangerous.[23]

Tourism has also added to the prestige of the *pedanda*. Many tourists come to Bali for a cultural experience. This usually entails visits to see the dance and drama spectacles, the painting and sculpture, but also the rituals and especially the cremations. During these the *pedanda* is on show and is the centre of attraction often surrounded by eager tourists taking photographs which may add to his lustre and prestige.

I would argue that the maintenance of the apex of the hierarchy is part of the reason for the continued relevance, integration and coherence of the rest of the caste system despite the criticisms increasingly levelled against it. Its twin pillars, now somewhat differently organised and related, are still entrenched not only in the hearts and minds of many Balinese, but also in the political and cultural life of the island. They provide a focus and a point of reference for the whole which would possibly fragment if they were to disappear, even if this focus simultaneously provides a clearly visible object on which to concentrate dissent.

Although this is not the place to assess the influence of tourism (Picard 1990a, 1990b), something should be said as to how it has affected status. Tourism, the dollars it has brought in, the push it has given to many cottage industries, and the impetus it has supplied to 'religion', has had a profound impact on Balinese society. There has been a dramatic expansion and diversification of the economy over the last 30 years, in part fuelled by tourism. People can now earn money, and for the fortunate few much larger amounts, from a much wider range of occupations than they ever could before. Since what attracts many tourists to Bali is the supposedly exotic nature of Balinese culture it is no surprise that significant sums of money are ploughed into the renovation of temples, into the paraphernalia of ritual which gets ever more elaborate and expensive, into the costly clothes and standard religious 'uniforms', and so forth. Of course money is also spent on many other things, but these all tend to take on a status dimension in the process (the cigarettes smoked, the beer drunk, the food eaten, the clothes worn, the motorbike owned, etc are all a matter of everyday conversation). Balinese may increase their spending on 'religious' items because it promotes tourism, but what is just as significant is that increasing income amongst Balinese enables status competition to penetrate into ever expanding areas, and increased inequality allows it to be taken to more ruthless extremes.[24]

Additionally, resources are diverted to ritual and religious endeavours because Balinese identity is now bound up most centrally with these activities. The perceived threat of Islam encourages Balinese to support Golkar and the present political regime, which has in turn validated Balinese Hinduism. The systemisation of Hinduism and the fact that other groups in Indonesia are converting to it is both a source of pride and a drive to further consolidation. Balinese increasingly define themselves as 'Hindus' and thus in relation to a series of practices symbolised by that label, and in opposition to Muslims, Christians and others. Whilst Balinese frequently equate the Balinese god with the Muslim god they also quickly point out the many problems of cross-religious marriages, the vastly different ritual practices, the absence of ancestor cults in Islam and its egalitarian ethos.

What constitutes Hinduism in Bali is not the existence of a series of texts, a Sanskritic philosophy, or a doctrinal great tradition, but rather the multi-layered ritual activities surrounding the temple system, wet-rice agriculture, the life cycle, the ancestor cult, and the unseen world of spirits and witches. Within this densely textured culture are positioned the high priest, powerful and influential descendants of the old kings, the *balian*, the temple priest and the *dalang* (puppeteer). All of these remain vital actors in the Balinese arena, and even if they have been joined by the bureaucrat, the businessman and the political party boss (most of whom are anyway embedded in descent groups, jealously guard caste titles, and participate in status rivalry), they have not given way to them. In fact the newcomers ratify their positions partly by reference to older values.

Furthermore the link between the past and the present (and therefore also the future) is continuously brought into the present in very concrete terms, by virtue of the immense importance to everyday life of the ancestors. In a very significant sense men and women never 'die', they merely change status and become invisible agents. From this much expanded world they are at liberty to intervene, with greatly increased powers, in the affairs of those left behind. The link with the past is also a source of guarantee for the future since it is the ancestors who reincarnate as new members of the descent group, and who legitimate or deny claims to higher status; they bring dreams, illness, unusual events, even cause fatal accidents to happen. The living must have these events interpreted by those with access to the unseen world. Such interpretations are spoken directly by the ancestors through the mouths of the medium and the *balian*, and hence are framed in relation to ideas and values which are continually being brought up from the past into the present. Such recycling can incorporate change as the mediums adapt interpretations to altered socio-political conditions.

Despite the appearance of a vast array of new offices and functions, it is Balinese, after all, who fill them, and they continue to live in a world we would call 'mystical'. It is a world in which far more goes on than can ever be directly apprehended. Businessmen, lawyers, policemen, politicians, teachers, etc. tell me stories about powerful *barong*, witches transformed into monkeys, *naga* ('serpents') guarding temples, and snakes biting those who pollute pure places. The state ideologies of progress and development, enthusiastically embraced by many Balinese, have gone some way in dislodging the ideas and institutions which dominate daily life in both town and village, but it would be a mistake to overrate this.

These institutions: status, *banjar*, temple groups, ancestor worship, language, ritual, and so forth, are not so rigid that they crack under pressure. They are highly flexible and adaptable to changing situations. They should not be viewed as substantive things which can be neatly pigeon-holed, but instead as sets of resources that may be put to use to meet changing needs and which themselves change as they attempt to meet new challenges. Status groups have been used as the basis for political party recruitment and business enterprises, and the *banjar* has been used for all kinds of development initiatives. These institutions are not mill-stones around the Balinese neck, but rather enabling forms of organisation of almost limitless flexibility.

Conclusion

In Geertz's remarkable analysis of the state, the *negara*, in nineteenth-century Bali (Geertz 1980), one of the issues which has repeatedly come in for criticism is his separation of status from power. According to Geertz the state was an institution designed not to govern, tyrannise or dominate, but to express itself in spectacle and ceremony. Power and authority were not delegated down the hierarchy but were surrendered up from peasant to lord: 'Power was not allocated from the top, it cumulated from the bottom' (1980:13, 62-3), and government was therefore a parochial affair conducted through local institutions, the village, hamlet, irrigation society, and voluntary groups. But there is a sense in which Geertz can be seen as having interpreted pre-colonial Balinese social and political organisation from a period, the 1950s, when the old ruling aristocracy had had power stripped from them first by the Dutch and then by the Indonesian state, in which latter of course they continue to maintain a large presence. Seen through that filter and from the position of a high-status nobility bereft of their traditional authority, Geertz's analysis begins to make some sense, since all that was left to the old rulers was their ceremony. Hence we get the picture of an aristocratic elite engaged in theatrical performance somewhat detached from the masses who organised political life. But this could be argued to be a modern product of profound changes read back into the past. What is clear from much subsequent research and from the material contained herein, is that the preoccupation with status and hierarchy was and is in no sense limited to the *triwangsa*, but is instead pervasive throughout all levels of Balinese society, just as in the nineteenth century the elite was a ruling elite. To be sure status is perhaps manifested more aggressively, expansively and stridently amongst upper groups, but that is an emphasis not a qualitative difference.

Status and rank are, however, not the only values in Balinese social life. Ideologies of collective or corporate equality are strikingly evident in many village institutions and in ritual and ceremonial practice. Ideas and values of equality and democracy are gaining ground all the time, but perhaps not as rapidly as some would like. Carol Warren has argued that equality and hierarchy are competing frames of reference. In one sense this is obviously the case. The *surya kanta* organisation (see note 4), the communists before 1965 and some modern day movements had, and have, as their aim, to eradicate hierarchy. Equally, many *brahmana* and *satria* loathe these ideas and cannot envisage a world in which status distinctions ascribed by birth are no longer important. For many in Bali, and especially the *triwangsa*, birth is vital because it connects one to a descent group and therefore to an origin, and to trace the origin of something is to demonstrate its truth (Schulte Nordholt 1992:28).[25] In other senses though these two ideologies do not compete but co-exist and complement each other. Just as the *déwa pikandel* of Corong try to resist the encroachments of the *ngakan* and to sustain a status distinction between them, they are themselves attempting to achieve equal status with *anak agung*. The Genteng *jaba*, willing to come to blows with those in their own *banjar* who now assert they are

41

déwa, have no problem giving due deference to, and recognising the status superiority of, authentic *déwa* in other *banjar* of the village. Disrupted death ceremonies do not appear to be attacks on the principle of hierarchy, except in unusual circumstances, but rather on new, inordinate and excessive claims to status that cannot be ratified in acceptable ways. The *jaba* of Nusa Penida who have become 'true' *déwa*, because they have established by divine intervention their real origin point (*kawitan*), have not tried to set themselves above their *jaba* neighbours except in so far as they have to carry out certain practices, such as using appropriate cremation offerings, now demanded of them by their ancestors. In all these situations hierarchy and equality appear to be two sides of the same coin; they constitute two perspectives on the same activity viewed from different positions; they do not so much compete as furnish contextually grounded tactical rhetorics and practices for achieving individual and group objectives.

If Balinese hierarchy was a dominant ideology which masked the real bases of power in the pre-colonial period (some men controlled land because, being the descendants of semi-divine beings, they were kings; rather than that they became kings because they gained physical control of the land) then indigenous notions of collective equality, which have begun to fuse with western notions of radical individualism, could be theorised as sources of resistance. Of course some groups, such as the *pandé*, have always objected to the claims of superiority advanced by high status Balinese, and no doubt peasants engaged in those petty forms of non-cooperation and disobedience that Scott (1985) has called the 'weapons of the weak'. But modern studies of ideology (for example, Bourdieu 1977; Scott 1985; Eagleton 1991) demonstrate that ideologies are not linked unambiguously with particular social groups in the way Marx and Engels (1965) envisaged. Ideological domination and incorporation are not simple processes but complex ones. One may call a system of ideas (though it does not have to be very systematic, and more than likely some ideas will be contradictory) a dominant ideology with the implication that it derives from a dominant class, but often enough the messages emanate from one's own class and articulate conflicts between groups within that class (Howe 1994). The same point can be made from a different perspective: an ideology is rarely the sole property of one group but should rather be seen as a cultural resource available to anyone who can use it, though clearly the prevailing power structure will mean that some groups are in a more advantageous position than others. Because an ideology is context dependent and has to make promises to those it subordinates (Gramsci 1971:161), there are always themes in an ideology which afford the weak a counter argument, and generally speaking this operates entirely within the confines of the existing ideology (Keesing 1982:217-31; Scott 1985:336-40). It is because Balinese ranking is so finely graded that the ideology of hierarchy supplies opportunities and rewards to almost all groups, even if it also provides a vocabulary for criticising one's superiors. Processes of status mobility and of forms of opposition to it are played out within the prevailing hierarchical set up. This is especially the case given that the values of hierarchy and equality are so closely related and intertwined. Notions and practices of equality should not be seen as weapons which unambiguously challenge hierarchy because, depending on the context, the assertion of equality (with a group of higher status, for example) may also be used as a strategy by which to press claims for superior status. In that sense ideas of corporate equality can be deployed as much within the framework of hierarchy as in opposition to it.

Obviously an analytical distinction must be maintained between Balinese ideas of corporate equality and imported ideas of equality related to western notions of individualism. The former have an intrinsic connection to hierarchy whilst the latter are antithetical to it. The coalescence of these has begun the process of re-working indigenous notions, particularly within the sphere of government and in the economy. This makes contemporary Balinese society a much more complex ideological terrain. The rise of new groups of entrepreneurs, classes of civil servant (including the army and the police) and low-caste wealthy landowners now compete with the old elites for political power, economic wealth and ritual status (in a way reminiscent of Beteille's analysis of a south Indian village over a one hundred year period [1965]), and in this enlarged arena and especially amongst urban intellectuals arguments for and against hierarchy and for and against equality now assume even more intense political overtones. Moreover, for thirty years, the Suharto regime, despite its denunciation of ideology and overt politics, has itself been promulgating its own very explicit ideologies. The foremost of these is the doctrine of *pancasila* as the sole foundation of the state (Mackie and MacIntyre 1994:25-9). But other ideologies have assumed almost equal importance and prominence. Those of development (*pembangunan* Ind.), progress (*kemajuan* Ind.) and a host of others are the basis for a wide variety of development projects (Warren 1993: Part III), and a large section of the school curriculum is devoted to inculcating the benefits and advantages of these ideas as well as to the creation of 'good' Indonesian citizens (Parker 1992a, 1992b). Ideologies such as these easily escape their original intentions and quickly find their way into debates about 'traditional' social organisation: the pretensions of the *triwangsa* hinder development; a modern society demands education, skill and aptitude to be rewarded more than mere birth; equitable progress is only possible if the different groups in Bali contribute their specific skills and knowledge. Balinese hierarchy, despite the changes it has undergone, has been very resilient up to the present day, but how it will weather the increasingly rapid social, political and cultural changes that are now sweeping the island is another matter entirely.

Notes

1. The sociological significance of the myth of the Majapahit conquest of Bali has received several different interpretations. The main issues revolve around which groups in Bali credit it with importance and which conceive of their origins as located in other mythical figures, the period in which the myth became relevant as a political and cultural charter, and whether the myth still has currency in contemporary Bali. For a summary of the main arguments see Supomo 1979, Schulte Nordholt 1986:11-14, Creese 1991, 1995, and Wiener 1995.

2. Schulte Nordholt (1986:31) denies that egalitarian society ever existed in Bali before the Dutch unwittingly introduced it.

3. There is now a vast literature on the emergence and development of nationalism, democracy and communism in Indonesia. Early accounts such as Kahin (1952) deal with nationalism, the revolution and the general political scene in Indonesia from the beginning of the twentieth century to the end of the Second World War. Mortimer (1974) has charted the rise and destruction of the communist party, but Kartodirdjo (1984) is a better guide to the rural unrest in Java during the peak of communist activity. The aftermath of the attempted coup in 1965 and the emergence of Suharto is documented in many books but Crouch ([1978] 1988) is perhaps still the best guide. On political conflict in Bali see Robinson 1988, Vickers 1989 and Schulte Nordholt 1991.

4. For a good account of these movements see Bagus 1969, 1975 and Vickers 1989:150-55.

5. Land reform in Bali in the 1960s was attempted but achieved only uneven success (Robinson:1992) since many land owners knew what was going to happen and had land registered in the names of relatives. During the Dutch re-organisation of Balinese villages high castes were sometimes absorbed peacefully and easily into commoner *banjar*, elsewhere they retained their aloofness from village affairs by forming exclusive high-caste *banjar* (Warren 1993:7-35). Picard (1990a:46) notes also that many noble courts integrated themselves into village affairs by surrendering their orchestras and dance costumes to *banjar* ownership.

6. Vickers (1989:170) describes the case of a very high status man in Klungkung whose cremation in 1965 became the site for a clash between the nationalists and the communists. Clearly here the principle of hierarchy was at stake and not merely the particular character of the deceased or his group, but this does appear to be a rare example.

7. Noise is very important at such ceremonies, including cremations. Depending on the interpretation noise can either distract spirits from interfering or it can help enlist their supernatural power to assist those carrying the very heavy tower. Often men shout '*suryiak! suryiak!*' urging the participants to yell and scream. In previous eras high-caste ceremonies often ended with gun shots and other types of percussive noise; and today the end of temple festivals, when the gods are being sent home (*budal*) or 'put away' (*nyimpen*), is accompanied by loud gamelan music and much shouting and boisterous jostling. On the opposition between noise and silence, confusion and order, see Vickers 1991.

8. Connor (1979) describes cases of corpse abuse in the Bangli region far more violent than anything I have

witnessed in Gianyar. In Bangli it is not uncommon for one group to make off with the corpse and, if they hated the deceased, to tear it limb from limb.

9. I am grateful to Raechelle Rubinstein for pointing this out to me.

10. For further information on the rise to power of Déwa Manggis in Gianyar, and for differing interpretations of his origin and therefore his status, see Geertz and Geertz 1975:119-24, Agung 1989:chap. 5, and Wiener 1995:239-46.

11. On death, bad deaths and cremation in general, see Howe 1980, Connor 1991, and Warren 1993:Part 1.

12. Connor (1982) provides the best and most extensive analysis of the different types and practices of *balian*.

13. In 1979 I came across a foundation legend for the village of Pujung in northern Gianyar which is a very interesting case of *saling alih* (Howe 1980:23-5). Given the prevalence of migration stories in Bali, both legendary and actual, and of cases of *salah kawitan*, it is surprising that nobody else, to my knowledge, has documented other cases of this fascinating process.

14. Such hierarchy is not confined to groups but indeed penetrates to the heart of family life. Men are considered superior to women in most contexts, as are husbands to wives and older siblings to younger ones. There are of course a great many factors, such as individual skills, personality, access to resources, etc., which complicate the issue of status ranking among individuals.

15. The literature on caste in India reveals a similar ambivalence. Some writers, taking a marxist perspective, argue that the predominant attitude of those in the

lowest castes is one of resistance or enforced resignation to the economic and political control of elites (for example, Meillassoux 1973, Mencher 1974). This links with up with criticisms of dominant ideology theories which argue that it is not ideology which creates value consensus and therefore social quiescence, but deeply unequal economic and political relationships which produce system integration (Scott 1985; Howe 1991). Other writers point out that brahmanical ideology is effective in legitimating the hierarchy even at the bottom end of the scale (Dumont 1972; Fuller 1988), and there are cases in which some untouchable groups are so pollution conscious that they have their own untouchables (Moffatt 1979).

16.   Other ways include becoming a 'powerful' person (*anak sakti*) such as a *dalang* (puppeteer), *balian*, temple priest, etc. Such people can help others, but also inflict severe damage through sorcery or curses. Yet another way is to become the recipient of a gift from god (*ica*) through being miraculously cured of an illness. Many such people become, to one extent or another, influential village actors.

17.   In relation to this point I suggest that sometimes too much is made of the generosity of the *banjar*. Corong is, in many ways, a modern village. Most of its high-caste residents are generally enthusiastic members of the four *banjar*, and the *cokorda* are evenly distributed amongst these so that each *banjar* has some representatives. High castes take part in the preparations for cremations and other life-crisis rites of their *jaba* neighbours, performing the same tasks, sitting at the same level, eating the same food from the same baskets, and so on. However, on the occasion of the death of a temple priest, whose family was too poor to cremate him immediately which is the customary practice since burial is polluting, the *banjar*

refused to give the family any resources beyond what was strictly obligatory. The priest was therefore buried for several years while the family accumulated the necessary wherewithal.

18. For an interesting discussion of many aspects of Balinese language uses, particularly in relation to the shadow theatre, see Zurbuchen 1987.

19. Patronage, nepotism and corruption are pervasive in the Indonesian economy and bureaucracy (Bresnan 1993, consult index under corruption, Schwartz 1994:chap 6).

20. Scott (1977) has made the general argument for Southeast Asia that pre-colonial, patron-client ties have remained important in the sphere of government and bureaucracy in the modern, post-independence period, even if they are less diffuse and more instrumental than they used to be.

21. In previous times tenants often only retained one-third, or even one-quarter of the crop, these days one-half of the crop is much more common.

22. Raechelle Rubinstein, personal communication.

23. In the pre-colonial period the relationship between kings and *brahmana* priests was very complicated. They were conceived as related to each other. Whilst there was often co-operation between them there was also a great deal of rivalry between them. Moreover their functions were nowhere near as clear cut and separated as the *varna* scheme seems to suggest. Although there are few examples of kings acting as priests, nonetheless kings clearly had a magico-religious aspect. What is well-known now is that *brahmana* priests were often rulers with subjects and who waged wars (see Worsley 1972;

Vickers 1984:27-8; Guermonprez 1989; Rubinstein 1991a, 1991b). It could be argued that since the period of Dutch colonial rule this relationship of tension and balance has begun to break down. The Indonesian state and its representatives govern Bali and have thus replaced the kings and their subordinates. But the *brahmana* priests retain much of their role. Indeed with the decisions of the Ministry of Religion relating to the status of Balinese Hinduism as one of the recognised state religions, and the advent of mass tourism, Balinese religion has to some extent been detached from Balinese culture and has become a kind of newly created autonomous mode of activity (Picard 1990b, Howe in press). Consequently the *pedanda* is more straightforwardly and unambiguously a priest.

24. This whole issue of the resources devoted to ceremonial activity is a very complex one. It has been convincingly argued by Connor (1991) that the last seventy years has seen considerable reform in cremation practices which have reduced both the costs involved and the time expended on this activity. Whether it is possible to make a similar case for other rituals and ceremonies is difficult to determine. It is my impression, however, that over the course of the last fifteen years, when tourism has increased at an exponential rate, Balinese have been spending increasing sums of money, not so much on offerings, as on new temple buildings (public and private), on formal clothing worn at festivals, exotic fruits and foods for offerings, on entertainments during temple anniversaries, new rituals not previously performed, and so forth. However, there are likely to be very great variations across Bali. Gianyar and Badung are the greatest beneficiaries of tourist dollars, and other areas of Bali have not fared anything like as well. But even in Gianyar there are staggering differences between villages only several miles apart.

At one point in her argument (1991:18) Connor argues that the increasing number of Balinese in urban, waged occupations makes short, simple, cheap ceremonies an attractive proposition. I have heard this expressed in Corong, but equally it is clear that growing affluence creates opportunities for status and wealth display. The family I lived with in 1993 were looking forward to carrying out a massive tooth-filing ceremony in the near future which would not only out-do anything they had ever done previously but, more importantly, put to shame their *brahmana* neighbours who had recently put on a lavish display when combining a wedding with a tooth-filing. Connor's argument tends also to ignore the enjoyment Balinese find in their numerous celebrations. Although many women complain quietly about the time and energy taken up by making offerings, and the income they forego (Nakatani 1995), nevertheless men and women alike eagerly anticipate their ceremonies and derive great pleasure from them

25.   The ideas underpinning hierarchy in Bali are not easy to get at. Asking Balinese what it is that makes members of different descent groups, and therefore different status titles, different elicits either no answers at all or answers which beg the question, just as would probably happen if westerners were to be asked about the basis of individual equality. The difficulty is trying to put the Balinese in the position where they find hierarchy puzzling, problematic and in need of justification. The most usual response is because people are born into different groups; it is one's ancestors (*keturunan*) which make the difference. And from there it is the origin (*kawitan*) which separates one group from another. But what is it about these origins which determine status differences? There appears to be no indigenous theory about the quality of 'blood' as there is, for example, amongst the Luwu of Sulawesi (Errington 1989). There are, however, several ideas about aptitude

51

and physical appearance. The children of great dancers and of ritual specialists such as puppeteers and high priests are said to be able to learn the skills and knowledge much faster and much more easily than those who have no such specialist in their immediate descent line. (This does not appear to apply to *balian* and temple priests who are recruited in quite different ways, usually through some form of divine intervention). There is therefore an idea of something being passed on but I have not encountered an explicit theory about this nor a mechanism by which it is achieved. High castes are supposed to have lighter skin (*putih*) whereas *jaba* are very black (*selem-selem*). The faces of *triwangsa* are said (by themselves) to shine (*caya, karat*) whilst those of *jaba* are dreary and indistinct (*mueg, urem*). The faces of children born to a high-caste man and a *jaba* woman will also be gloomy. Such representations are not used in public in my experience. Once again the bottom line appears to be origin/descent and it should be understood as a cultural axiom.

References

Agung, I.A.A.G. 1988. *Bali pada abad XIX.* Yogyakarta: Gajah Mada Press.

Bagus, I.G.N. 1969. *Pertantangan kasta dalam bentuk baru pada masjarakat Bali.* Denpasar: Universitas Udayana.

Bagus, I.G.N. 1975. Surya kanta: a kewangsan movement of the jaba caste in Bali. *Masyarakat Indonesia,* 2, 153-62.

Bailey, F.G. 1971. Gifts and poison. In his *Gifts and poison.* Oxford: Blackwell.

Barber, C.C. 1979. *Dictionary of Balinese-English.* Aberdeen University Library: Occasional Publications No 2, (2 vols).

Barth, F. 1993. *Balinese worlds.* Chicago: Chicago Univ. Press.

Berger, P.L. & T. Luckmann. 1967. *The social construction of reality*. Harmondsworth: Penguin.

Beteille, A. 1965. *Caste, class and power*. Berkeley: Univ. of California Press.

Boon, J. 1977. *The anthropological romance of Bali, 1597-1972*. Cambridge: Cambridge Univ. Press.

Bourdieu, P. 1977. *Outline of a theory of practice*. Cambridge: Cambridge Univ. Press.

Bresnan, J. 1993. *Managing Indonesia: the modern political economy*. New York: Columbia Univ. Press.

Connor, L. 1979. Corpse abuse and trance in Bali: the cultural mediation of aggression. *Mankind*, 12, 104-18.

Connor, L. 1982. *In darkness and light: a study of peasant intellectuals in Bali*. Unpublished PhD thesis, University of Sydney.

Connor, L. 1991. Contestation and transformation of Balinese ritual tradition: the case of ngaben ngirit. Paper presented at the Artistic Representation in Social Action Conference, Princeton University, 8-13 July.

Covarrubias, M. 1937. *Island of Bali*. London: Cassell & Co.

Creese, H. 1991. Balinese babad as historical sources: a re-interpretation of the fall of Gelgel. *Bijdragen tot de Taal-, Land- en Volkenkunde.*, 147, 236-60.

Creese, H. 1995. In search of Majapahit: defining Balinese identities. Paper delivered at the Bali in the Late Twentieth Century conference, Sydney University, 3-7 July.

Crouch, H. 1988 [1978]. *The army and politics in Indonesia*. Ithaca: Cornell Univ. Press.

Dumont, L. 1972. *Homo hierarchicus*. London: Paladin.

Eagelton, T. 1991. *Ideology, an introduction*. London: Verso.

Errington, S. 1989. *Meaning and power in a Southeast Asian realm*. Princeton: Princeton Univ. Press.

Friederich, R. 1957. *The civilisation and culture of Bali*. Calcutta: Susil Gupta.

Fuller, C.J. 1988. The Hindu pantheon and the legitimation of hierarchy. *Man*, 23, 19-39.

Geertz, C. 1980. *Negara, the theatre state in nineteenth-century Bali*. Princeton: Princeton Univ. Press.

Geertz, C. 1983. *Local knowledge*. New York: Basic Books.

Geertz, C. & H. Geertz. 1975. *Kinship in Bali*. Chicago: Chicago Univ. Press.

Geertz, H. 1995. Sorcery and social change in Bali: the sakti conjecture. Paper delivered at the Bali in the Late Twentieth Century conference, Sydney University, 3-7 July.

Gramsci, A. 1971. *Selections from the prison notebooks*. London, Lawrence and Wishart.

Guermonprez, J-F. 1987. *Les pandé de Bali: la formation d'une caste et la valeur d'un titre*. Paris: École Francaise D'Extrême-Orient.

Guermonprez, J-F. 1989. Dual sovereignty in nineteenth-century Bali. *History and Anthropology*, 4, 189-207.

Holt, C. 1970. 'Bandit island', a short exploration trip to Nusa Penida. In J. Belo (ed), *Traditional Balinese culture*. New York: Columbia Univ. Press.

Howe, L. 1980. *Pujung, an investigation into the foundations of Balinese culture*. Unpublished PhD thesis, Edinburgh University.

Howe, L. 1984. Gods, people, spirits and witches. *Bijdragen tot de Taal-, Land- en Volkenkunde*, 140, 193-222.

Howe, L. 1989. Hierarchy and equality: variation in Balinese social organisation. *Bijdragen tot de Taal-, Land- en Volkenkunde*, 145, 47-71.

Howe, L. 1991. Rice, ideology and the legitimation of hierarchy in Bali. *Man*, 26, 445-467.

Howe, L. 1994. Ideology, domination and unemployment. *Sociological Review*, 42, 315-40.

Howe, L. in press. Kings and priests in Bali. *Social Anthropology*.

Kahin, G.M. 1952. *Nationalism and revolution in Indonesia*. Ithaca: Cornell Univ. Press.

Kartodirdjo, S. 1984. *Modern Indonesia: tradition and transformation*. Yogyakarta: Gajah Mada Univ. Press.

Keeler, W. 1987. *Javanese shadow plays, Javanese plays*. Princeton: Princeton Univ. Press.

Keesing, R. 1982. *Kwaio religion: the living and the dead in a Solomon Island society*. New York: Columbia Univ. Press.

Mackie, J. & A. MacIntyre, 1994. Politics. In Hal Hill (ed.), *Indonesia's New Order: the dynamics of socio-economic transformation*. St Leonards: Allen and Unwin.

Marx, K. 1970. *Capital*, vol. 1. London: Lawrence and Wishart.

Marx, K. & F. Engels, 1965. *The German ideology*. London: Lawrence and Wishart.

Meillassoux, C. 1973 Are there castes in India? *Economy and Society*, 2, 89-111.

Mencher, J. 1974. The caste system upside down. *Current Anthropology*, 15, 463-93.

Moffatt, M. 1979. *An untouchable community in south India: structure and consensus*. Princeton: Princeton Univ. Press.

Mortimer, R. 1974. *Indonesian communism under Sukarno: ideology and politics, 1959-1965*. Ithaca: Cornell Univ. Press.

Nakatani, A. 1995. *Contested time: women's work and marriage in Bali*. Unpublished PhD thesis, Univ. of Oxford.

Parker, L. 1992a. The creation of Indonesian citizens in Balinese primary schools. *Review of Indonesian and Malaysian Affairs*, 26, 42-70.

Parker, L. 1992b. The quality of schooling in a Balinese village. *Indonesia*, 54, 95-116.

Picard, M. 1990a. 'Cultural tourism' in Bali: cultural performances as tourist attraction. *Indonesia*, 49, 37-74.

Picard, M. 1990b. Kebalian orang Bali: tourism and the uses of 'Balinese culture' in New Order Indonesia. *Review of Indonesian and Malaysian Affairs*, 24, 1-37.

Poffenberger, M. & M. Zurbuchen. 1980. The economics of village Bali: three perspectives. *Economic Development and Cultural Change*, 29, 91-133.

Reid, A. 1988. *Southeast Asia in the age of commerce 1450-1680*. New Haven: Yale Univ. Press.

Robinson, G. 1988. State, society and political conflict in Bali, 1945-1946. *Indonesia*, 45, 1-48.

Robinson, G. 1992. The economic foundations of political conflict in Bali, 1950-1965. *Indonesia*, 54, 59-93.

Rubinstein, R. 1991a. The brahmana according to their babad. In H. Geertz (ed.), *State and society in Bali*. Leiden:KITLV Press.

Rubinstein, R. 1991b. Alliance and allegiance: the case of the Banjar war. Paper presented at the Artistic Representation in Social Action conference, Princeton University, 8-13 July.

Schulte Nordholt, H. 1981. Negara, a theatre state? *Bijdragen tot de Taal-, Land- en Volkenkunde*, 137, 470-6.

Schulte Nordholt, H. 1986. *Bali: colonial conceptions and political change, 1700-1940*. Erasmus University: Comparative Asian Studies Programme.

Schulte Nordholt, H. 1988. *Een Balische dynastie: hierarchie en conflict in de negara Mengwi 1700-1940*. Unpublished PhD thesis, Free University of Amsterdam.

Schulte Nordholt, H. 1991. *State, village and ritual in Bali*. VU Amsterdam: University Press

Schulte Nordholt, H. 1992. Origin, Descent and destruction: text and context in Balinese representations of the past. *Indonesia*, 54, 27-58.

Schulte Nordholt, H. 1993. Leadership and the limits of political control. A Balinese 'response' to Clifford Geertz. *Social Anthropology*, 1, 291-307.

Schwartz, A. 1994. *A nation in waiting: Indonesia in the 1990s*. St. Leonards: Allen and Unwin Pty Ltd.

Scott, J. 1976. *The moral economy of the peasant*. New Haven: Yale Univ. Press.

Scott, J. 1977. Patron-client politics and political change in Southeast Asia. In S. Schmidt, J. Scott, C. Lande & L. Guasti (eds), *Friends, followers and factions*. Berkeley: Univ. of California Press.

Scott, J. 1985. *Weapons of the weak*. New Haven: Yale Univ. Press.

Supomo, S. 1979. The image of Majapahit in later Javanese writing. In A. Reid & D. Marr (eds), *Perceptions of the past in Southeast Asia*. Singapore: Heinemann.

Tambiah, S.J. 1985. A reformulation of Geertz's conception of the theatre state. In his *Culture, thought and action: an anthropological perspective*. Cambridge, MA: Harvard Univ. Press.

Tsing, A.L. 1990. Gender and performance in Meratus dispute settlement. In J.M. Atkinson & S. Errington (eds) *Power and difference: gender in island Southeast Asia*. Stanford: Stanford Univ. Press.

Vickers, A. 1984. Ritual and representation in nineteenth-century Bali. *Review of Indonesian and Malaysian Affairs*, 18, 1-35.

Vickers, A. 1989. *Bali, a paradise created*. Berkeley: Periplus.

Vickers, A. 1991. Ritual written: the song of the Ligya, or the killing of the rhinoceros. In H. Geertz (ed.) *State and society in Bali*. Leiden: KITLV Press.

Warren, C. 1993. *Adat and dinas: Balinese communities in the Indonesian state*. Kuala Lumpur: Oxford Univ. Press.

Wiener, M. 1995. *Visible and invisible realms: power, magic and colonial conquest in Bali*. Chicago: Chicago Univ. Press.

Worsley, P.J. 1972. *Babad Buleleng*. The Hague: Martinus Nijhoff.

Worsley, P.J. 1979. Preliminary remarks on the concept of kingship in the Babad Buleleng, In A. Reid & L. Castles (eds), *Pre-colonial state systems in Southeast Asia*. Kuala Lumpur: Royal Asiatic Society.

Zurbuchen, M. 1987. *The language of Balinese shadow theatre*. Princeton: Princeton Univ. Press.